Sister

SISTER

Poems

Nickole Brown

RED HEN PRESS | LOS ANGELES, CALIFORNIA

Sister: Poems

Copyright © 2007 by Nickole Brown
ALL RIGHTS RESERVED

No part of this book may be used or reproduced in any manner whatsoever without the prior written permission of both the publisher and the copyright owner.

Book design by Mark E. Cull

Quoatations are from the following sources:

Kinnell, Galway. "Oatmeal," from *Selected Poems*. Northumberland, U.K.: Bloodaxe Books, 2001.

Maso, Carole. *The Room Lit by Roses*. Washington, D.C.: Counterpoint Press, 2000.

McHugh, Heather. "From 20,000 Feet," from *Hinge & Sign: Poems 1968-1993*. Middletown, CT: Wesleyan Poetry, 1994.

ISBN: 978-1-59709-089-6
Library of Congress Catalog Card Number: 2007925347

Published by Red Hen Press

The City of Los Angeles Department of Cultural Affairs, Los Angeles County Arts Commission and National Endowment for the Arts partially support Red Hen Press.

  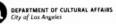

First edition

ACKNOWLEDGEMENTS

Grateful acknowledgment is made to the editors of the following journals in which some of these poems (or versions of these poems) appeared: *32 Poems, Another Chicago Magazine, Chautauqua Literary Journal, The Florida Review*, and *Post Road*.

Many thanks to all who made the writing of these poems possible through their friendship, mentorship, and support, especially Lori Kay Scott, Lynnie Meyer, Maryrose Smyth, Mark Pickett, Jerry Chang, Raymond McDaniel, Laure-Anne Bosselaar, David Jauss, Victoria Redel, Tom Lux, Miles and Mimi Coon, Tony Hoagland, and Cynthia Arrieu-King. I'd also like to thank those who saw this manuscript through its many incarnations, offering their invaluable suggestions along the way: James Kimbrell, Mary Ann Taylor-Hall, James Baker Hall, Dick Allen, Debra Nystrom, Peter Conners, John Hoppenthaler, Beth Adler, Gretchen Henderson, Adam Day, Zeke Buck, Douglas Goetsch, and the coffee-chugging members of my Monday-night poetry group—Erin Keane, Emma Aprile, Zachary Bramel, Martha Greenwald, Teri Whitehose, and Troy Alvey.

I'd also like to extend my heart-felt gratitude to The Kentucky Arts Council, to The Kentucky Foundation for Women for believing in me for over a steady ten years now, to the Virginia Center for the Creative Arts for giving me a delicious six-week stretch of uninterrupted time, to Brian Grady and Kathleen Flynn for the cover art, to Annie Langan for the nifty website, and to all the kindness and guidance I could ask for at my home-base, Sarabande Books, particularly Sarah Gorham, Jeff Skinner, Kirby Gann, Kristina McGrath, Jen Woods, and Jeannette Pascoe.

Finally, I would like to thank those who've never given up on me through all my moody scribbling, especially Christopher Baker, Leslie Wilson, Pam Swisher, Clay Marshall, Ginny Tabutt, and Ryan Trauman.

For my mother
because nothing could keep me from her

Contents

Sister

PREFACE

Sharon oldsy?

Sister, we come from
water we made ourselves
with the suckle and swallow of our unmade
bodies submerged in a sac so sweet
with our vestal piss that we breathed it,
formed trachea and kidney with it,
our soft faces forced
forward with the game of fist
and thumb, our heads
without a thought of skull
bracing her

placenta with one prayer—*stay*—
until we grew enough
to kick her
skin up into a sheet tent
in the night.

Here is a flashlight,
give me your hand, together
we will make shadows:
hook your suckling thumb in mine
and wrist to wrist
we'll silhouette an angel landing
on the caul, that shimmering
webbed cap of good fortune
once sold for shillings to sailors
who pocketed the afterbirth talisman
to keep from drowning.

I tell you this story because it is
the story we need

to believe our offal is divine,
the worst of our darkness
a darkness ringed
in battery-powered, plastic light
but *light*, God damn it, see it, there—
fluttering with finger-tipped wings,

light nonetheless.

I

We are two hearts, four arms, four legs, two brains, four eyes in one body. . . .
As if I were not strange enough already—now, this eight-chambered heart.
—Carole Maso

twins/
siblings/
children
conceived
+ growing
"simultaneously"

FOOTLING

We have heard her tell the story
over and again, like this: an early spring
tornado, a still, yellow sky,
nuns who said *must have felt better*
going in than it does
coming out as they gave her
a hot compress and dimmed the lights
for pain.

She was half my age now, sweet
sixteen and barely healed
when God smacked half the trees
flat and she curled down
under a mattress
in an empty bathtub
in an empty apartment,
a newborn suckling
the tips of her fingers. The porcelain,
cool white womb, had a drain

ready to carry anything
it could swallow to the swollen
brown Ohio, and though the tub
was dry, she used her heel
to flip the drain open, asking
the river to take it, all of it,
especially that moment the month before
when she didn't know better

but to sit up and grab the slippery blue
feet first, an impossible breech, a twist
with a snap that meant

conjecture or conclusion?

leg braces, special shoes, a grown woman
who would never walk right
in red heels. Frightened in this storm,
she wanted the tender word

birth but knew better now. *Birth*
meant forceps, rips, umbilical cords
wrapped around the neck. *Birth* kneaded
the abdomen for more birth, recovered
with douche singed with a drop or two of Lysol,
boiled a set of glass baby bottles in the same
pot that made the pinto beans. Not much more
to hold and so she touched
the blue leg of her bruised baby, cooed
footling, thinking it sounded
more like the name of some imp
than a complication, *footling*, her shape-shifter
sleeping inside the cup of a trumpet vine,

footling, because she was so young
and who could blame her, dreaming
away and waiting while wind
tore the silk of clouds to shreds,
plucked off pieces of home,
peeled shingles back from rooftops
one by one.

How She Conceived

I.

Count nine months back.
Find *June*,

find the foxfire summer,
find mama's fifteenth year,
a dark undergrowth
of fern and fertile knots of water
moccasin down at the creek,
high, green, and indifferent

to the trying of her new
softness in a concrete slick
basement where cave crickets
fiddled in the moldy dark,
or on a rooftop where shingles
gripped her, black grit catch
on her tender bare—

anyplace where nobody could hear,
nobody could catch her,
nobody could switch her ass on home.

Or better, because you know her
well as I do—giggling, cigarette sneak,
miniskirt-hike girl she was—
where somebody *could* hear,
or barely hear: a custodial closet, knocking
splash of mop water running gray,
a velvet movie seat, hinges up
and creaking, or my choice:

an empty baptismal font
hidden behind stained glass,
strong sun spilling
blue and red and orange and
blue across my daddy's back
and one praying pink
hat in the front pew, *God love her*,
fanning with a folded program,
old clip-on pearls
deaf to their kissing sighs,

oh, the hot repentant air.

II.

And you, sister? You know. Done
respectably. Ten years later, in a bed.
Soft moaning, flat-backed, missionary,
a warm rag and a glass of water to follow.

Imagine bright rods of moonlight
cutting through blinds to stripe
his back, and her pillow cool to the touch,
flipped after a nightmare to try to put her
back to sleep.

Her panties are folded and cotton,
his pinkest skin smells of soap,
an amber stereo light shadows simple,
familiar things: his watch, wallet, mess of change,
her earrings, bracelets, discarded blouse,

a dog stretched unbothered,
dreaming at their feet.

There is a fan too, the spinning
set on low, and after she stares at the burst of blades
until they disappear, blinks her eyes
to strobe them back again.

Later they know you are coming
through ten-dollar home tests,
one line going one way and
another line going the other.

1979

That year was the cyanide hiding
in the stone of a peach. Look, how yellow
the photographs, a nicotine sheen
on our happy days, a disease roiling
out of the Congo to lay flat the tender
men before I learned to spell
their names. Eric, for example,

Erique, with that surprise ending
to match his frosted tips, or Chris, now
Chryss, his name changed from a Bible school
salute to something that rang like a wet finger
rimming a genuine crystal glass. They came

from the casserole-fed dredge of Kentucky
to click and sashay through the salon
where mama doused perm solution on old gray
and I sorted yellow rods from pink,
where mama cut a wet ridge held between
pointer and middle and I swept it up,
where mama waxed her own eyebrows
clear out of existence and I pushed
pins into a Styrofoam wig head, always

terrified she might change
her hair so much she'd be
unrecognizable, impossible to find in the dizzy
spin of racks at the mall. That was when
the shop was filled with nothing more than disco tunes
and (if ever was such a thing) simple childhood
fears. It was another year before

she got herself a diamond and dropped
her scissors in the neon blue for good, leaving

right before the wake of purple sores,
all those men I adored abandoning
their hard-ons through the holes of walls,
the vending machines of fruit-flavored lube
emptied in filthy gas station stalls, the hubcap
chained to the key reflecting
a future tasting of either latex or
death. But I swear to you—when Chryss

sat mama down to dye her
hair and I began to cry, he quit,
put the bottle down. And Erique, he
scooped me up on his fat lap, said *girl,*
wild horses wouldn't drive that crazy mama
from you; besides, I promise we'll
keep that bombshell
blonde. I pressed into his body—
he was soft bruised fruit—
and I was blessed to ever know
a man's flesh could feel sun
warm, smell peach sweet.

KEEPING THE LIGHTS ON

When he came, mama and I were front porch girls
eating lemon wedges with salt, barely making it

through one Saturday morning cartoon
before the set blacked out, the single white dot shrinking

to the middle of the screen. When he came, I colored
with cheap crayons so waxy they left more

of a grease stain than a mark, and hippie girls came over
dripping their long rivers of hair

over guitars to sing *salvation army counters, tea and
oranges*, how Jesus sank *like a stone*. When he came,

we were poor, but empty
in an open field with nothing to find

but each other. We ran across it
as if we had red kites to lift off the ground, and

exhausted, giggling *ashes ashes,*
fell down.

When he came, she smelled
all wrong. I slept in my own room but could not

sleep for their noise, and when I went down the hall
to knock, to make sure she was okay, I was stopped

by the bright band of light,
the yelling yellow line under their closed door.

WEDDING PHOTO

She is Saturday night
fever silver and acrylic
heels to match. For bouquet,
a mesh clutch just big enough
for lipstick, lighter, twenty
bucks cash. For veil,
braids of smoke, and for brides-
maid, a sulking six-year-old
yanking down a too-tight ponytail.

He is poly-pressed, moustache
sheik, his corvette waxed,
packed, ready to go.
On opposite walls

two gilded
mirrors face each other:
an old story—new family
smiling and waving at an eternity
of reflections, each one
slightly smaller,
all the same.

What happens when you alter shape — center the ? poem.

25

STICKY FINGERS

Unborn we   listened.

We were covered
with an okra fuzz of hair   fed cravings
of white bread   fried chicken   tomatoes
straight from the can   all through
a pulsing straw a braided beam of light
to our navel.

After we shook
with her cigarettes   vibrated with the underwater
drone of that album
that fascinated me—
its *real* fly-zipper cover   the one that opened
to a black-and-white photograph   grainy shadows
of a man's rock thin hips
in tight, dingy underwear.

That was me at six   my fascinated hands
quiet at the pluck
of each brass tooth   from the other
hiding with my stash
of raisins   crayons   a Barbie with her thumb
chewed off
          closet closed tight.

But unzipping   no matter how slow
rips loud like twisting open
a church peppermint   so afraid
mama's new husband would hear

like he heard the autumn leaf quiet
of his magazine pages   turned
through the bathroom door
     with my eyes submerged in
that sea wreck and anemone of
     oil slick women only in boots
     oil slick men only in tool belts

a woman with legs spread wide to the white of fast water.

I was caught   album cover zipper
half down
     the needle scratching
     the empty space
before repeat.

     He crouched down asked
Want to see more?   I said

nothing.   There was no
answer.   The best I know is that
you don't know this.   The best I know
is that you heard a different music:
not hers   not his
     but mine——

     you hummed
cassette tunes played over and over
so loud that the silence in between songs
popped with static electricity biting
like a bug light waiting to zap.

You were busy sealing up your gills   losing
your tail   tending to everything the unborn
must suffer   all to the submerged   rattle
of half-blown speakers.

I could say I was playing the music
for you
                    but I wasn't.
                              But I can still say it,
still want to have wanted to——

playing loud for you
cranked all the way up cracking
the windows   driving my stepfather
mad   because
                    yes   my baby
sister   yes   you were still safe
in there
                    in her
your unformed ears
          tiny blossoms
budding from your head.

A Cup of Anything

Sister, this is not
a code. These words
are not to be spoken.
This is the way
I'm able:
describing everything
but. I know
you don't know
me and I know
I know the cat
better than you.
How can you

forgive me as I've spent
more time trickling
water between the fat
leaves of my jade plant
than brushing your hair?
That I recall serving
the shaking girl
who came in on Tuesdays
coffee with
one cube of ice,
one cube of sugar,
and a straw
she had to drink through,
but I've never poured
you a cup
of anything

I can remember?
All I can tell you

is that when you
were new
the crown of your head
broke my heart
with the smell
of sweet, warm
bread.

JESSICA MEYERS IN THE CORN

I sat Jessica on a construction site
pile of white rocks, said, *pull your pants
down, feels so good, so warm.* We found

a refrigerator box and some old darts.
She said, *we'll play magic, you be the woman
cut in half, I'll be the moustache
man throwing knives.* I tied her

to a lawn chair with jump rope, said
*I'll knot your wrists and ankles,
see if you can get free, if not, I'll torture you
with ice and ivy, drips of hot
milk, then you can do me.* We played

house, *I'll be the mom and you be the dad*, practiced
how she moans and how he grunts. We took turns

climbing into the dryer to roll in the tumble
cycle then put on our roller skates and played
dance, a centrifuge of silly, hand-in-hand
spinning until we shattered
through a tabletop of glass. In puddles of seeping

groundwater, I plugged in electrical cords and her skin
burned black. She said, *let's recite Bible verses,
write everybody down that's going to hell.* I said *okay,
let's pee on the side of the house.* We did all this

then ran into the corn. In the red dirt
we found each other—
panting and afraid, alone.

WHAT I DID

I.

Once, I slipped into the small bedroom
with the large waterbed and opened wide
mouths of diaper pins for you,
a baby who was to come.

I pushed sharp ends through thick
rubber the color of a prosthetic arm,
sunk the needle down into the mattress
then pulled up tiny bird-streams,
arcs of water that had endured
their tossing for four years.

I watched the stale water pulse
upwards, happy to see their bed
stung by a hundred bees, pricked
with the spindle of a hundred
goodnights, a witch's welcome
slowly filling the moat, their bed
empty and hard, their clean sheets
white flotsam, ghost-ship debris.

Your Water, Breaking

I.

When you were curled as an unsprung fern
unblinking   a fixed fiddlehead on blood-
rich walls
I overheard mama talk
        the white coil of the telephone
stretched flat round the corner
        her face running beige makeup
into the secret
                whispering receiver.

She said *Seven, probably.*

Said *As soon as he gets home.*

Said *Fried chicken, cornbread, sliced tomatoes, salt.*

Said *He's so picky, I know, spaghetti sauce,*
        had to strain every one out.

Said *No, not even green peppers.*

Said *No, wouldn't touch that with a ten-foot pole.*

Said *I know, no man*
        is easy.

Said *But why?*

Said *No, plum tired*
        but not far enough along to tell.

Said *Was a blessing, maybe,*
> *my baby not even two, still in diapers,*
> *still wore bells on her shoes.*

Said *Remember? Wore her out with a*
> *switch, she kept running off, got bells*
> *so I could hear where she was.*

Said *Yes, tried again last year.*

Said *Just God's way, I guess,*
> *telling you the baby ain't right.*

Said *Thought I'd never stop bleeding,*
> *just a round light, then out.*

Said *Like in the movies,*
> *I swear—count back from ten,*
> *you get to six, wake up forty-five minutes later.*

Said *Thought I'd never stop bleeding,*
> *bout bled to death.*

Said *Enough of that.*

Said *Better slice the potatoes,*
> *almost six now.*

Said *Yes, and I know it.*
> *Need a separate skillet for the onions.*

Said *Yes, yes, yes. I know.*

II.

The miscarriage before that
       I saw myself
       thought
       a newborn
       mouse
floating
where no mouse would go.

The marble bathroom swirled
       in lavender and slick
red, their newlywed
       lace-trimmed towels—just for guests,
       not to be used—mopping it up,

then the indecent flush
       the open mouth of the toilet
       indifferent
       not ashamed of taking
whatever it could get.

III.

So you were her fourth but second to be born,
so wanted, *so careful* she did not pick up
clumps of clay his boots left on the porch,
so careful did not Clorox the floor,
so careful did not reach to the chipped plate
top shelf, did not bend
to paint her toenails seashell, mocha, spice.

So careful did not run but walked, her hands
on the small of her back, that perfect *V* from behind
that made her arms a set of wings—
mama chickie chicken, mama cockatiel angel, we teased.

So careful did not drink, not once,
I swear, the wine coolers
unopened next to the catsup in the fridge.
So careful, her feet elevated and iced, her legs rubbed
free of charley horses and cellulite, and your daddy,
saying *careful now*, holding her at the elbow
over the last of the winter ice, saying *careful now*
reaching to the chipped plate
top shelf, painting her toenails
seashell, mocha, spice. Everything
careful now. Everything not to dislodge you,
not to noose the cord, always to bring your head
down into place. She took long hot baths,
slow walks down the drive,
then because we cannot expect her not to be
her, smoked cigarettes at the mailbox,
looking out over its little red flag.

She was cussing, balancing
a full Pepsi on top of her bare tan stomach
when the water broke and joy
flowed from her, dripping down
through a click-in-place
lawn chair in the sun.

A Heartbeat Pillow Too

For you, he sped
down the emergency lane
then spent sixteen hours pacing
long white hospital halls
in squeaking tennis shoes.

For you, he bought me
a blue tee-shirt that read
I'm The Big Sister Now
across my unformed breasts
and a book that said
it would be ten days
before you could make your own
tears despite all your crying,
and despite all your crying
you'd been crying months before
this with two tiny, seaspun lungs.

For you, there was pain
medicine shot straight into her spine,
stirrups cushioned with pot holders,
pills to dry her up,
bottles with disposable bags of milk,
pills to make her flow, pumps to do it for her—
nipples spreading plump and brown.
There were stitches that dissolved
on their own and a softsong nurse
in latex gloves who stitched
a routine incision that kept one hole
from tearing into the next.

For you, there were mittens to keep
your long fingernails from scratching

yourself, needles that pricked
your ankles with vitamin K,
an incubator where you waited
like a dumb tomato on a windowsill
for the liver-yellow to fade. At home,
he had a room freshly painted
for you and in it was a battery-powered
pillow he bought that mimicked
a heartbeat to trick you into thinking
you were not born yet.

WHAT I DID

II.

In the squealing creak
of a yellow school bus
I made baby feet
in the morning fog windows,
the side of my fists and ten
thumbprints down.

I wiped them away, breathed on the glass,
made others
with higher arches, rounder heels,
perfect going-to-market toes.
I wiped those away, breathed on the glass,
tried again, then wiped, breathed,
tried again,
then again.

MORO REFLEX

You came home bawling, colicky, dispositioned
bad, a mess of black tar meconium then green
shit and spit up and hot yellow running down
my side. Mama says you screamed before your body
was even all the way out of hers, that you worked your
angry pink lungs as she pushed and you hadn't quit

fussing since. So when you dozed across my lap
that afternoon, she cooed *see how that baby takes right
to her sister, see how good she'll be*, and I sat in holy communion
silence charmed by the tiny rise and fall of your
speckled chest, imagined touching the vulnerable
fontanel, the forbidden raisin of your
umbilical cord still gauze-taped to your waist.

I had quieted you somehow but with no
swaddling and nothing to hold you
tight, it didn't last—you jerked back, cracked
a panicked, shivering cry. Embarrassed, my charms
gone, I wondered how you could be born fearing
you'd fall, how mama, quick as a blue jay
snatched you from me, terrified
I'd let you drop.

It Is Possible He Thought

It is possible he thought
he loved me. It is possible
he wanted me
glistening in gold
lamé and muffed in white
fur, it is possible he braided
my pigtails after showing me
this and that
and exactly how fast.

It is possible he mesmerized me
with mouth tricks: a dragon spit
of lighter fluid throwing flames into the air,
bangles of smoke rings breathed to fit
my skinny wrists, the fire put out by flicking
his empty cheeks to make the insomniac sound
of water night-dripping into a sink. He then
showered, and smelling of fresh cigarettes and
blue soap, asked before entering, stopped
when I cried hurt.

It is possible he bought me,
games with men made of pixels, marbles, plastic
coins, but the object was always the same:
eat or be eaten, eat as much as you can.
I then got a vinyl pop-star jacket,
dozens of zippers to catch every flyaway
hair, and a three-story dream
house where I hid away
the weekly allowance, ten dollar bills
stuffed into all the home's hollow spaces—
the white columns, its hard blanketless bed,

I even pulled apart the doll bodies, crammed
full the doll legs.

It is possible the year before
you were born he quit me
and I drew fourth-grade pictures
of swan necks coughing up
eggs into the womb,
that I scored an *A* by memorizing
test in *testicle*, *fall* in *fallopian*,
saw *public* to be one slender letter away
from curling in his rank and humid dark.
I knew the answer but wanted to see
if he'd tell the truth, so I asked him
how babies were made, cloyed the question
with bellybuttons, a pink or blue stork.
He said *I just wanted to give you*
a sneak peek, a head start.

Nights he would unroll his
blueprints across the kitchen table, whisper,
See this? With this I can buy you a hundred
red bicycles lined here to there. I imagined
chrome gleaming, the handlebar jet stream
of yellow and orange flaring, fast-pedaling far
beyond the long black drive.

POLTERGEIST

With cable t.v. and nothing more
to do, I watched her
so many times—that porcelain
girl, kneeling in innocent night-
gown white, her hair clean and straight
as an untouched sheet
of ice. I wanted to be her, my hands

pressed against the tinny pings
of ghosts beating themselves like moths
against the screen, my tongue close enough
to lick the hairs of static electricity
from the glass. I wanted the dead
to beckon me with curling fingers
come, I wanted the opening
of the closet door to twist me
in a tornado of light. I wanted to go
but mostly I wanted

a mother to notice I was gone, to call and call
after me, to follow the unknown path
snatching me back from the beast, to land
jellied red in her arms, our faces
exhausted, hieroglyphed
with a pulp of flesh that read
one word—*born*.

previous poem (s)

WHAT I DID

III.

I dressed the toy
poodle he gave me
up like a plastic doll.
I painted his clicking
toenails pink, pulled
four manicured paws
into the arms and legs
of your terry sleeper,

cut a little hole
for his wagging tail
then put the baby bundle
into the wastebasket,
dared him to tip it over.
When he did, *bad bad dog,*
back to the trash you go.

Other times, I bowtied
his apricot ears ruffled
in a Sunday dress,
fed him candy until he
slicked the rug
and while mama scrubbed
I picked him up
by the scruff, drug him
out back,

whipped him until his yelp
sounded round the block and
echoed back for more.

44

if you don't quit that hollering,
I'll tie you to the garage door and
flick the open switch,
I'll swaddle you up
in duct tape, tuck you shut
in a closed
dresser drawer.

Ghost Dog

I wasn't a bad
girl. I could be
coloring-book
quiet, dressing dolls
behind the couch
and putting all the pieces
back before bedtime.
I did things
because

I don't know

why, not
for the slosh and groan
of them through the wall,
not for the double-dog dare
boy who dropped
his jeans to the ground
after school, especially not
for the
ghost
I saw, tiger-pawed,
transparent
as wet tissue, eyes
like flashlight in a white
possum's face.

Even if I were
to try to tell
you now why
it would be
a list of everything

in the basement,
crammed with
model airplanes
meant to fly
       over us
making shadows
of crosses
on green fields while
       your father controlled
flight
with a black box
in his palm, his work-
bench of hot
glue guns, pencil-shaped
knives, blonde
wood light as Styrofoam
with moon marks
of my fingernails
and your biting
baby teeth,
a small iron used to melt
thin sheets of color
onto the skeletons
of wings. But that says
       nothing.

I might as well say his
television, a glowgreen corner
spreading out as the picture
died, the remote
under his chin.
I might as well say his

too-white
tennis shoes, the long stairwell
down he Cloroxed
clean of my smudge
fingerprints, his coffee can
ashtray, his blueprints, his plastic
comb, his diesel chugging
pickup, his, his, his
his, his
             it
             doesn't matter.

The only thing that was
             mine
down there
was the stupid
             ghost—guard dog, spirit
animal, canine Casper
hallucination, what-
ever. Howling
silent star, and I swear:
transparent white
shadow like wet
tissue, unblinking eyes
a flashlight in a white
possum's face.

It paced the ceiling,
silent, watching, not doing
a thing
for me.

PINWORMS

I woke
with the sheets
back,
my underwear
down, and
mama using
two fingers
to spread
me apart.
When I
jumped
she clicked
the flashlight
off,
said *just checking,*
they only crawl
out of you in the
pitch dark,
don't you worry
yourself now,
then finding nothing
she was
gone.

THRUSH

A songbird word, yes, but also a white growth of yeast
> across your suckling tongue.

Cat lurking, a little blue gray flash sprung up from the wheat,
> but also mama's breast, a mastitis streak of hot bruises, bloodless nipple, blocked
> ducts, milk pumps, wet rags.

A featherless hatchling, throat gulping chewed bits of worm,
> your white mouth red-shrieking in my arms, rooting on my still-flat chest,
> wanting to be fed.

Little bird, little crier,
> I had nothing to give. And knowing how everything I was
> cleaved, I tried to lullaby you, but couldn't sing the part
> about the bough. Out of song,

I set you down to fend for yourself, stepped away thinking
> I'd never be anything more to you than
> an axe, a knife, a slingshot snapped back into the blue sky.

TRAILER PSALM

After I understood what happened, I thought
my clit big as a donkey's ear, that pink
pulse of pleasure thick as a thumb
stuck out on the highway,
asking just anyone to pick me up.

After I understood, I found how to make that ear
sing myself—a handkerchief rocking side to side
       in the film-strip dark, the hard plastic
       calf of Barbie's leg, the fin of a bath-time shark
       slick with the orange slip of shampoo.

I was shellacked in shame, and in his work trailer
       parked in the driveway when he wasn't
       out of town, I hid to masturbate and
       pray. I read King James there, chanted
       cursed be he that lieth and *wicked*
       thing from Leviticus and Deuteronomy
       until I choked, felt the tingle of hellfire

licking the tiny seat of the flip-down tweed
       bench. I read the Begats from beginning to end,
       and wearing homemade haircloth underwear
filled with hamster litter   paprika   and hills
       of fire ants,
       I forced myself to sit still
until I wrote each and every word of it down.

To beget—*to procreate, as father or sire*, as in one
       begat me then another begat you, as in Seth,
Shem, Milacha, Cain
       as in first there was light and then came

lots and lots of sex
           as in walk into the valley of the shadow
of darkness   fear   the little aluminum
light   in its hard circle sits   a sweating
           child   in her hand   an oversized pencil copying
           letter by
letter   trying to write   her way
           out.

II

The foetus,
expert at attachment,
didn't dream that
cramped canal would open
into sound and light and love—
it clung. It didn't care. The future
looked like death to it, from there.

—Heather McHugh

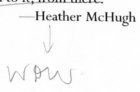

THE ROOT WOMAN

A black woman worked for pay on Friday
to feed you mush pears and mush peas
and to teach me how indigo paint and colanders
keep out haints, how uncut hair and unshaven legs
retain strength, how a red ribbon, a brass key and fire
brought love.

With her, the growling ghost of my childhood
did not return, and your daddy disappeared for good
into the basement, building model airplanes
and bluing himself with late night flickerings
of television to put him to sleep. She protected me,

lioness she was jumping down
barefoot to crack clams off the canal wall and eat
them with hot sauce right where she stood, red running
to her elbows. She flushed chitlins for dinner,
a garden hose running the dark flecks out to settle
soft into grass. And fried chicken, marrow
sucked straight from the leg bone.

I held hot rags to my breasts when she said
it would make them grow, imagined
a red bra, a fast blue motorcycle, a boy's fast black hair
flying back into my mouth. Two years later she left
and they came, early enough and barely there—tender
swells with airbrush-pink nipples. It was then I stole
mama's cigarettes, the ones she wasn't supposed to be smoking,
and smoked them out the bathroom window, my lips pressed
to the grain of the flyspecked screen. I changed

my wardrobe with a handful of rubber bands
and a gallon of bleach. It was a poor girl's tie-dye, sister,
because we were poor: all of the rings
a faded version of the cloth's original,
purple on blue, red on orange, a stained-glass shirt fit
for my own make-believe stained-glass father, worn tight
to sneak out to the asphalt black, crushed glass
twinkling under street lights. I met one with blue eyes there,
watched him spit tobacco in the air
then catch it on his tongue.

What I Did

IV.

On the first day of my first
period, I had to ask mama
for a pad, and while she called all her
friends and cried *my baby's
grown,* I walked head down

humiliated through the weedy
field, slid through a barbwire fence
straight to a neighbor's neglected
pool where water was stagnant
still and milky green. There I stripped

naked in the sun and
sunk, not splashing but floating
face down, pretending I was
drowned and opening my sex so
the blood would tempt some

tentacle or tooth from the bottom
that could not be seen
to drag me under and seal my legs
shut into one glamorous tail, to cover
the worst part of me with scales
big as buttons, shimmering belly dance

coins, the muscle under the new
waterproof skin
useful and strong.

JOKE

We have been taught how
to button up, close the blinds, lock the doors
good and set the alarm. We know to call
when we get there, we flock in groups,
go to the bathroom in pairs, walk alone
through the parking lot looking dead
straight ahead carrying mace.
We have been told

men can sniff us out, catch us
unaware, so like frightened animals
burying scent
we hide our waste, that blood
incapable of clotting
that drips red then brown, we wrap it
twice in toilet paper,
squirrel it to the bottom
of the can. Because she said

only a girl who doesn't know no
better would humiliate her daddy
with a smell like that, because his punch-
line as he flipped the steak
on the grill and gave the neighbor a wink
was *I don't trust anything*
that bleeds for five days
and lives.

TINTINNABULATION

What did you hear with a wooden spoon in your

                                                fist, running into my room to ring

the xylophone headboards of my brass bed? What did you hear

                     in the echo of hollow poles, the gold flaking off onto the floor?

Was it music

                           to you, a home safe enough to be as loud as you want,

humming along and whacking your little stick?

                                 Did you sing the he-kissed, she-kissed

song I taught you, the couple in a tree and

                         later their baby carriage? Did you jump the bed

springs flat, kick a speaker in, rip the head off a tiger

                         and run singing *run, run as fast as you can*?

Did I holler,

                         twist your ear? Or did I roll my eyes and pop

gum, pretend you'd disappear?

                                     No, this despair

is too much, let me ask it

plain—sister, did you feel loved, ever,

by me?

THE SMELL OF SNAKE

Few memories, those years
besides the smell of dead
kittens under the car and the cucumber
of copperheads crisping
the creek where I waded
with a net from our above-ground pool
to scoop up black tadpoles and crawdads,
the adrenaline flash of minnows silvering
an orange bucket. Few memories
of you, nothing to say about

you learning to roll over or sit up
or crawl, and by the time you toddled
down the hall to reach my door
it was locked, shut with a finger-
smashing slam and a sign barred
with exclamation points that read
Private Get Out. I was hoarding

a stash of precious, breakable things,
things you weren't allowed to touch—a boy's
speed skate laces and his sister's stolen
champagne flute of Mardi Gras beads,
a wind-up ceramic ballerina balancing
on one chipped toe, raspberry-flavored
lip gloss and soft plastic bracelets worn to look
like a slut. In two summers,

I had gone from the creek to the all-night
seven-to-seven skate, I had gone
from the freckled giggle pop kiss to the tongue
down the throat, I had learned what acid-

washed jeans can do for a girl, especially
when she learns to skate
backwards, the smooth-footed eight curve
side-to-side sway of her hips.

The kids I knew, like me, all came
straight from the mud, and with legs still
mosquito-pocked and the smell of snake
in our hair, we struck our father's
lighter in one hand and held out
our mother's aerosol in the other,
sprayed *fuck-you* balls
of fire into the air. We wrote *ozzy rulz*
across our eight punch
knuckles, carved our desires
into wooden desks; we passed
notes and played hooky and told stories
of schoolyard rape done
with broken bottles and broom
sticks. We were

afraid, and like a pack of hungry
dogs, we marked
each other—safety pins and blood,
scratched things like *best friends*
forever then vomited
bile into the mud.

What I Did

V.

When you were five, I took a
thing that was yours, a jar
of fireflies you spent all night
plucking from the gloam, and while
you hollered from the locked side
of my bedroom, music and smoke curling
under the door at your feet,

I set the bugs loose in the dark, pretended
constellations I could identify,
fairy clusters of wishes I might
make, thumbs held high above
the crowd, turning the little wheel
of their lighters, thumbs
burning for an encore song.

Hearing you, I cranked the stereo
louder, and when that didn't work,
I took the pencil-hole punched foil,
the careful top you made for your
lantern world, balled it up
and threw it at you as you ran
crying down the hall.

TELL ME

A coloring book
Sesame Street
I think
and you had drawn on
Grover's and Elmo's
crotch
enough
to show
that you knew
what monsters had
down there.

Sweet burr, this
is love
that blisters—
when I saw that
I knew I was
no sister.
Tell me
but do not
tell me it
happened
to you?
Tell me any
old thing—

a kissing cousin
closet playing
nurse, a neighbor
boy show-you-
mine-if-you-show-me-
yours, a late night

movie snuck while
everyone slept,
please, any
thing, most
any
thing
but him.

TRESTLE

I gave the best of my body's
new beauty to boys
in basement bedrooms, the walls
sweating groundwater behind posters
that turned electric green under black
lights. Upstairs, always some lump
of a mother clicking overhead who
sold makeup to earn a pink
Cadillac, and a father, usually
drinking but always pissed, who
dropped the coin of his heart into
the red envelope of Tet and threw it
away with everything else
from Vietnam. We clung

to each other——the boy and
I——first trying the gentle hippie
daze watching spirits rise
from the tips of incense sticks
then sick of being underground
with a wild barnyard kitten
that shit the couch, we shrouded
ourselves in black from head to toe and
snuck out to spray paint anarchy
signs on clean, white walls.
We clomped our combat

boots through the old tuberculosis hospital
and screamed out of broken windows
through ivy vines and spiderwebs, and
finding what we thought were body
chutes, we pretended dead and

jumped down. We walked train tracks
smashing pennies, spoons, keys,
we dangled our tired feet high above
from the rusty bridge and did not hold
hands in a parasuicide skydive

but simply looked out
on suburbs and strip malls
under humid white sky, the black
woods' edge sometimes flashing
with deer at the littered shore
of two ribbons of light, one coming
toward us and another
already gone.

Trestle

POP

I never could call him
with the authority of *father* or the affection of *daddy*
but settled on *pop*,
an easy sound—pop-
corn, pop-goes-the-weasel, popping your cherry, your pills, a bright balloon,
what other word spelled backwards as forwards
with as much innocence as experience, simple
as chewing gum and as confusing as him, walking in the back
door after a long day's work and I say *hi,*
pop,
best I can and he says
nothing,
goes straight for the basement
door, stepping down quiet into his nicotine blue?
Press your bottom lip
under your top,
feel that little ball of air,
roll it around your mouth,
expel it in one
syllable
and tell me
I didn't try.
Come on
now,
tell
me,
tell
me
I didn't?

Barren Lake

Because I was a teenager and it was a family vacation,
I threw things: unripe pears picked straight from the tree

smashed against the cabin, a Japanese beetle stone-skipped
across the hood of the car, a Styrofoam cooler of half-dead

half-live minnows
making a mercury of the grass.

After, I kicked things—door jams, rocks into water—then made
a redneck halo for myself by tying a June bug to leftover fishing line,

let it buzz circles above my head. All the while,
your father, dressed in underwear and a gold toe ring,

sunned himself in the boat, and later at the table
he let me know he saw me swimming and acting up on the shore, said,

I couldn't stand to see you in that little bikini,
all those bumps and cellulite,

and as I picked the croutons from my salad
I thought of the hundreds of hooked hybrids

swimming at the bottom of the lake,
pierced and pissed and unable to breed themselves,

special man-made fish from a farm to fill the waters
just for this—the hunt,

creatures perfect in size and speed
and with red reef gills for a taxidermist

to spread wide. I thought of my girlhood, how I was the catch-
of-the-day, how I was once a lean nymphet

swimming in the cradle of his fist, how even then I waited
arched on a plaque for someone to come

and spray the gold back onto my dead body
to make it perfect again.

The Choice

I.

Sister, let me say it. I was
Krishna blue with worry.
I grew heavy
with a smear of life, possibility
of a knot forming
a ropy cord for its own
blood. I read the Greek *hystera,*
meaning *womb*, meaning
wandering, untethered, free
floating in panicked flips,
but I couldn't listen to that—
I knew the uterus was nothing
if not an anchor, potent barnacled bottom
of the most mediocre sea—
tender, resentful nurse, our
        lonely, beholden mother.

II.

It would have pushed
my belly, my breasts, my future
forward. Magic, yes—glands
that will turn sweat into
milk, bones that will open
like creaking gates, skin that will stretch
every pore to grimacing
until my navel was flat, my past
let go. With child, I could have conjured
a seed to grow much faster

than it would in water
soaking it in a cup
of my own piss.

But later that baby
would want to know.
What would I tell her?
Some hot white lie
on sheets right out
of the dryer? A big fib
on the old shag rug, dandelion lint
exploding across the living
room floor? Or would I give her
a glimpse of the party, bubbling
with bong, pipe, and tattoo
of crow, the boy with the slightly
crooked nose and nothing

more to remember him by?
You've never known
what it is to guess, to walk
through the dark
alleyways hand-in-hand
with an imaginary father,
pretending his feet alongside yours,
pretending his step
over broken bottles,
his boots grinding the sharp
glass into white resort sand.

WHAT I DID

6th
of the
seven

VI.

I went
Wednesday morning,
I knew what to pack:
warm socks, a robe,
sanitary pads.
I needed insurance
papers and a fake
license too, proving
two months past legal,
a first trimester check
for $650, nothing eaten
after midnight, no colds
or fevers for a week
before.

And here's what
I left behind:
the brochure photo,
a pencil pointing
to an unborn hand, fingers
so short that they couldn't yet
touch but simply radiated
out of the palm
like a tiny, red sun.

Wasp, Bear, Abacus

So what if the woman   your father first wanted
to marry   was killed in the melting
fiberglass cage   of his first white corvette?   So what if
she died   quick enough   not to complete her last
thought?   That her son did not die   but slipped into a slow-drip
coma   waking   eight months later   barely knowing
how to walk?

                    When he married mama, the new
          car still had paper tags, and twenty years later he
               talked the boy's aunt into letting him take her
                              from behind.

So what if   his father was   a Korea Vet
and after two decades   of drunk
picked up   his twelve-gauge   sawed-off and blew
a black boy's   jaw   into a confetti   of buckshot and flesh
          to scatter the grass?   So what if
                    the reason
                    was rape,
a cliché   sodomy   of dropped gym-shower
soap, the locker vents   tiger-striping his Davy Jones face?

          Even if the kid who did it was big and mean and
          black he used it to fill his hate mouth with a lifetime
     of *that nigger this* and *that nigger that*, never once naming
               the name of the one disintegrated, pulped
                    to mulch on the suburban green.

The point   is not   if we are   to believe him,
          because even liars
                         tell the truth.

                                   The point is that the man was a wasp
                                        defending his dry nest
                    of desire, driving his rusty barb deep. The man was a grizzly,
                                        breaking the cub made
                              by another to open the sweet cup
                                   of estrus that would yield
                              his own young. The man flipped

                                        his abacus, counted

every   bead of pain
          to add up
          to *excuse*,

                         then pardoned himself every easy spring that came his way
                              dropping her pink blossom panties to the ground.

Go ahead,
believe him.
                    Sometimes I even do.

Pity him,
          take a hot coal
from the fire   and burn this   into the fence:

                    Criminals are made.
                         Not born.

Put your ear to his

                    heart to hear a four-thump beat
                        of *shitshit*, *shitshit*, his blood
            diesel fuel and red clay, his veins not pumping
                        evil but weakness, the spill
                        of a man who simply

        cannot stop.

SOMNILOQUY

Mama sleeps, her body curled tight
      like the sole of a house shoe hot from the dryer.

Mama sleeps, her bent knees bare, her ankleted
      ankles crossed, one foot on top of the other, stacked
      placid and limp, Jesus-style.

Mama sleeps, her jaw knocking all night on the same
      closed door, her canines worn flat with the pop and grit
      of chewing a thing impossible
      to swallow.

She doesn't like heavy things on her, nothing to weigh
      her down, so with one thin sheet she sleeps, her
      hand to her face making an *L* with her pointer
      alongside her nose and her thumb tucked under her chin.

At first you think it's a vestige from some crybaby
      comfort time, but look closer, see how the hand steadies her
      pretty dreaming head, how it holds her pretty pout mouth,
keeping it shut.

NIGHT-BLOOMING CEREUS

I should have
moved out
later but couldn't leave
soon enough.
Early as I ever
could since the day
he moved in, dropped
a yellow crayon down
his jeans wanting
to play.
Come-n-get-it,
he said, and
I did.

I should have
gone
but where to and
too late
the day she began
to swell with you, sick
on the smell
of my perfume.
She sat
on the steps crying
into an old tea towel,
asked *you wear it*
on purpose, don't you
and *why you got to make*
things so hard
on your mama?

How could I
barely have left
you even when
I did,
birdleg thin,
your asthma machine
kicking up fog,
a mist to open
like a cactus flower
I saw once—
white petals that only
unfolded in full glowing
moonlight, light when things
were supposed to be dark.
And you,
on the counter, heels
swinging the cabinet door,
wheezing as you breathed it in,
wheezing as you breathed it out,
waiting for
your lungs
to bloom.

What I Did

VII.

I packed everything,
crammed it all
steering wheel to trunk,
the car windows a slide show
of every girl's high school years:
cassettes, tampons, blue jeans,
prom carnations dried upside-down
held "together forever"
with hairspray,

nothing, really, but everything
I even knew I could
own. A boyfriend wearing the same
dirty shirt he wore every day
sat up front holding the cage
of a yellow bird
you and I both loved.

If you were in the driveway
I didn't see you,
a seven-year-old knock-kneed kid
kicking gravel nowhere
with the side of your bare
foot.

I was in that white car—half tank of gas,
loud muffler ready to drive North fast,
no apologies,
no saying
goodbye.

III

maybe there is no sublime,
only the shining of the amnion's tatters.
—Galway Kinnell

Riddle, Riddle, Marie

Pretend I know you. Pretend in a deep pool
I always find you first following the familiar
Marco-Polo of your voice. Pretend we've played
freeze-tag wrapped in the sticky transparency
of spring, new grass greening our shoes and knees.
Pretend we've played hopscotch, made it to heaven
so many times we wore the chalk to a knuckle-scrape
nub, that we kicked the can, jumped double-dutch,
sat cross-legged facing each other clapping out
dirty songs about boys. Pretend I know something

and point it out. It is not red, that color quick
to disappear without light, and not blue, that satin shade
of drowning. No, orange is violence and yellow
fear, and purple, no, it's an obvious
iris, a flower church-dusted, bearded petals snapping
shut. No, pink are the walls of a bedroom
long gone, and white reflects everything
lost. We are older now, try for shades

not taken, hues we never got to see,
all those school words that meant
nothing until it was seen to be believed—
milkblue Adriatic, dustmoth brown
storm, oilslick eel crushed underfoot in Chinatown.
Whisper expensive green—chartreuse, peridot,
olive—or new paint for new walls—Wrought Iron,
Derby Rose, Queen Anne's Lace. Show me what patterns

you see on the pressed insides
of your eyes, and I'll return with the colors of where
I've been all these years—rust smear of roach in

tiny apartments, yellowed plastic
computer clicking through the night,
rain in the canals, pastel squares of chicklets
sold for a peso by such a tired little girl. Tell me,

what is it you don't see? Sit with me, sit in
grainy black, we'll be like two sisters
leg-locked, up too late playing slumber party
game after game in the flashlit dark.

Speak & Spell

Of course I always did spell it wrong.
Cause there's no way to speak and spell things right,
especially after all those years
washing with a *wursh* rag, frying in *earl*, stuffing
my drawers in a *shiffarobe*, settling down into a *pilot* on the floor.

And it's true, I got up in front of a crowd, said
suck-ee-yent when I meant *succinct*, wouldn't have known better
if not for my boss, red-face ashamed: all those words I'd read
but never heard out loud, all those words we made our own.

Go home, sister. Open the kitchen drawer. It's the only place
you'll find a thing to write with: maybe one of his drafting pencils,
too square to roll and sharpened with a knife, maybe a stick of her eyeliner,
greasy kohl brown. Or maybe, under napkins, coupons, and catsup packs,
you'll find that crayon I always used, the daffodil color of spring
and so short you have to peel back the last of its paper, have to hold
it with the tips of all your fingers to get anything down.

I want you to write *pedi*, as in *get those baby's shots at the pediatrician*,
as in *the whore got her toes painted red*. Then scratch out the *i*,
the singular eye, because the point-of-view doesn't matter anymore,
because vowels are tricky—*it's already ate a'clock*, we might say, *way past time*.
Add an *o*, because the *o* is a mouth, empty and round, a number multiplied to make
nothing. Then add the word *file*, as in his cabinet, always locked,
never mind what's inside, then change the *f* to *ph*, those two secret consonants,
whispering into the phone. The rest is game show simple: take an *e* and *end it*.

Who knew there was a word for it, much less a right way to write it down?
Pick up that crayon again, show me what you've learned,
make this into a word, make it a note left behind. Know the good
thing about yellow—it's so light, she'll never see,

and to make sure, write it on something she'll read
but read over—a grocery list, a receipt, a Christmas card from me.

ONTOGENY

It's the science of everyone's earliest days
first plastered across the cover
of *Time* in 1965: unborn children
lifted from their dark organ
warmth with scalpel and scope, carbonation
blown to float them up
to the flashing fiber optic eye.

Nine years later even the first
footsteps on the moon was old
news so it was no big deal for a young
girl in Kentucky to flip the pages
tracking her swell from clot
to snail to kicking feet before labor brought
something substantial enough to make
a shadow, to recognize that shadow,
to fill an urn full of its own ash.

Not that mama ever cared
to look. *You got fat, then you had a baby*
was all the learning she sought, the rest
of what she needed to know was
hot rolled into her bleach blonde hair and
plucked into an arch, never once wanting
to read about her own bones that once began
growing outward from the middle,
hardening from the crosshairs out,
the origin of core implying an axis
of tough, the apple seeded central
with poison, her earliest memories deepest
and the least she's likely to admit.
And she'll tell you: *back then,*
you had to lay it down, let it go,

never mind what the doctor and schoolteacher
say, never mind that she came from a long line
of men who break things, of children
who hid under a bed, a tattletale stream
of urine making them easy for him to find.
She knows the worst of it, she knows everything,
but the weight of knowing must be shucked:
there are shirts that need starch,
shelves that need lining,
simple, dim salads to toss with iceberg and carrots,
jars of imitation bacon and milky dressing on the side.

Look in the garage, sister. Even it's been cleaned
top to bottom, not a spider egg or rainbow
drip of oil in sight,
it is Godly, scrubbed spotless,
all our tears swept from every corner
with a cheap straw broom.

ONE HUNDRED AND FIVE TIMES

everybody just wants to get

        over it. everybody just wants

                  to move on. he was good

to you. he put you through

       college. and we've gone over this

              105 times. you know what

your biggest fault is? your biggest

       fault is blaming people for not

           reacting the way you do, the way

you want them to. you need to put

       the past behind you, to quit

           dragging this shit up

every chance you get.

           everybody just wants

    get

    over it.

          everybody wants to move on.

            he was good

put you through

            we've gone over

            this

            105 times.

   your biggest fault your biggest fault
   blaming people for not

            reacting
            reacting
            reacting
            react

            the way
         you want. past behind

quit dragging
shit up

to get
over it.
to move
on.
he put you
and we've gone

over
this
105 times.

your fault your fault your fault your fault your fault
everybody
wants
everybody
wants to

he was good
he was good
he was good
he was good
he was good
he was good
he was good
to

put you through college.

we're over this
dragging.

just want to get
over it.

just want to
move on.

he was
105 times.

he was
every chance.

you know what
you know
fault? your biggest
people not
reacting, you
want them. you need
the past, quit
this shit
every chance.

everybody just wants.
everybody just wants.
what he was
to you. he put you through

105 times.

91

WOODEN DOLL

Tell it from the baby's point of view,
the doc says, and I try:
I was born but never really
alive. I was wooden, but porous, breakable,
cheap, balsa—the kind of wood light enough
for toy gliders and kites. I was a boy
child, but as they only had dresses for me,
that's what I wore, passed back and forth
between each tickling admirer
wearing yellow ruffles and lace.
I was left
on a bar while my mother was almost raped
and made her quick side-door escape.
I was taken to my grandmother's house
where my uncle carefully swaddled me in pink
then forgot me,
I was half-lost under couch cushions
smothered under everything that needed to be vacuumed out—
dog hair and change and popcorn.

I was submerged
in a spill of water
and drowned there,
and when my mother came back
to rescue me, she didn't do CPR but simply drank
from me, sucking the water from my nose, mouth, and eyes
then spit it all out on the floor.
She could never tell if I was revived because
I was never really alive. Stubborn, she kept checking
my breathing anyhow.

What the dream teaches
is this: if I were born a boy,
I would have known none of this.
It took years to reach through
those wedding cake ruffles to find my own sex,
and when I did, it was atrophied
like a bound foot that no longer knows
toes from heel, the flattened arch
more mollusk than human, all that unused skin
folding round the center
looking like a wet, cardboard rose.

Simply put, when I am asleep,
fear keeps the breast's milk
from dropping down—
in dreams
I am the mother
and do no better
than our own.

Know the Sound When You Hear It

I drew dirty dick stick figures and shoved
them under his steaming shower door
years before I learned cicadas belonged
in trees and crickets on the ground. I then snatched
his bath towel and tripped giggling with it

dripping down the hall, but please, understand,

> this was before spring was spring and I was
> silent, barely familiar with the air or how it stirred
> after the watermelon was cut and I was handed
> a cracking wire of fire for the Fourth of July.

I still don't know how it happened or how I could
love anything now, especially such noise—

> it's nothing but the rattle of prong
> tongues and distended throat, the hitch and rub
> of barbed legs, brittle lace wings, come-
> fuck-me calls, the self-crushing insect breast.

My point is this: you grow up, read the facts,
but rarely can you be sure.

> A child will tell you the very trees are
> chirping, talk talk talking
> the summer away, that the brown bark throws its voice
> like a puppeteer and for that she's sent
> wheeing into the air, sweetsonged for saying it so.

But that same child will sit on the edge
of her mama's body-scented bed, tell how her
stepfather would sit in the middle

of a blue satin comforter and she'd pretend
ice skate around him wearing nothing
but nylon socks and out of the cave

                steps the hydra of ignorance, snapping nine
                        toothless jaws.

Maybe there will be
a call to him, a confrontation enough
to splatter his vomit on the phone booth glass,
but otherwise it's a slur of her easy syllables—
                      forget
         it, let it go, get over it, let it lay, move on, wash it down.

Listen to the summer air, sister. The truth issues
a jittering, sorrowful sound.

                              If you want to console
                              me, nod and smile, say

         yes, invisible flea orchestras, little
      leafy bells, a hum of humidity to soothe you, mercy
        found in the thick cricketing night.

How to Forgive

plant it in the folds of your intestines
where it is warm and dark and swimming
in shit. keep it there in the churning wormed
organs, hold it still, claim it your own. say
this is mine—my garbage, my rot, my rage, and I will not
just lay it down.
rock it in your arms and love it till it calms, rub its demon head
with sweet oil and song, find its facula and stare unprotected into sun.
call your body
home.
make room without throwing a single thing out
to clutter the world. you are not mercury for the mouths of fish,
not a plume of smoke to lift hollow bones. do not throw it
like a bottle from an overpass onto a speeding car, do not wait
for it to seed as you wait tentacled in sleeping beauty's hair.
listen to me, I know how it works, simply
bury it, but bury it
alive.

In Winter

Helplessness
crouches
next to the orange glow
of a space
heater
from January till May.
Look
through the window
all you want,
but all you'll see
is a square of steel,
the nerve-ending trees
feeling little
through days
long and brown.

The seasons,
either mosquito
lush or dead
wood, are like
the architecture here—
Victorian or prefab, not much else
in between, the valley brought
to its knees
by drive-thrus and strip
malls, car lots of primary-
colored triangles
flapping in endless dinge.

The mud
is thick, like a mix of dog
shit and deer blood,

construction sites so deep
in suck earth
that the men throw down
two-by-fours just
to walk across. Your daddy brings
that clay

home on his boots
so bad
you can scrape it
with a spoon.

You can hear him
coming a mile down,
gurgling sound of diesel,
the silver silhouette
of two big-tittied girls
flashing on his mud
flaps, and in his immaculate king
cab, an ashtray full of change and one
empty coffee can
for cigarette ash.

In winter, it is all
fried bologna: there is no
work, and when there is,
he works
so hard he can pop
open the skin of his knuckles
by making a fist. It's then
he slathers his hands
in Vaseline and sleeps

wearing kitchen gloves.
Full of endless spring,

he talks about
enough money
for red bicycles, toy poodles, hot tubs.
Full of endless spring, he buys
mama things
he can't afford,
some things she doesn't even
like——that mink stole
round her pretty shoulders,
a tacky grandma
glam she only wore to church, the tiny
bead eyes in its dog face
glinting at me as I pretended
to pray. *Well*, she said, petting
the little dead muzzle,
least he tries.

CHRISTMAS

I know I didn't come home
again this year, but I did come
close, came all the way out to the place
that sells trees in the parking lot
between the fast food joint and super store.
You know the one, a fence strung up
with bare bulbs the size of fists, all the trees
roped sloppy, their starless tops pointing
every direction but up, a semitruck
with an open gate selling
mottled oranges, unshelled peanuts, peppermint
poles, jogging pants.

The woman who stepped out
of the sleeper cab was another one of those
could-be-pretties, rubbed raw by wind, and
her hair, dyed three shades
too light, floated two inches above brown
root, the white tips disappearing into winter
sky. She says, *I'll give you*
that tree there for thirty.

These trees are thirty dollars? I ask.
No, I said I'd give YOU
that THERE tree for thirty, her voice gritted
with hate—to her, I am a snot, a faux
fur, an artsy-fartsy Holly Hobby from
Bardstown Road. *I can sell some trees now*
for cheap, she says. *Do you hear?*
For cheap. I feel poverty's

contagion come over me,
like I'll catch something
if I stay too long, that I'll turn
again into a kid clutching
a doll that does nothing special
but close her eyes
when you lay her back.
I start to leave when
I'm stopped—a reindeer head
dressed in baseball cap and tie, hung
on a wall plaque. What's more, he's
animated, singing "My Old Kentucky Home," and
under him a woman propped
in a wheelchair
laughing and singing along. Her skull
comes up through her face
fierce like a spring bulb, she is green, almost
gray, her complexion the shade
of *just a few weeks left*.

Sister, I am ashamed to say it
but I was frightened—not of death
but resignation, the acceptance
of *enough*, gifts wrapped under a tree
with its bad side pushed
to the wall, the holiday
jar of hard candy
stuck in one multicolored lump.

NAVEL

Before we were born,
we had every cell
of every egg
we'd ever have.
Think, sister:

our mama carried within her
any grandchild we'll ever try
giving her, any towheaded, spoilt-rotten kid
we might conceive too late in life
walking the tiptoe tripwire
of an ovulation calendar, our most
modest parts up in the air
in some upside-down aerobic bicycle position
we liked as kids but isn't
so great now.

Everything goes back to her:
those cells
within cells
within cells,
all encased by one
painted doll, her pelvic frying pan
belted in disco gold, her biscuit-brown waist
roller skating with a princess belly chain
that swung metronome time down the street,
that sweet stomach of hers
she covers
with a washcloth when you come in to talk
while she's taking a bath.

Next time,
watch her,
she'll do it,
lay that white rag
right across her middle,
keeping it warm maybe or
hiding it,
scarred as it was then with a zebra
stripe of stretch marks,

porn-queen flat as it is
now with the new cowlick
belly button the surgeon gave her,
a cinched knot that gives her away
like a tiny silver sticker does
an expensive, real-looking
silk rose.

And I can't help but miss the old one,
the original castaway,
can't help but wonder
when she rejected the innie she had,
the one her mother gave her,
to buy herself a new one
along with two grapefruit breasts
that do not fall
but buoy
when she reclines into the soapy water.

Her old navel is gone. Gone
who-knows-where,
out there,

a dead star
that we call dead
only because it's not giving off light.
Pay attention—it's pulling,
it lives, still has gravity,
yet we orbit
this new one
despite ourselves,
regardless,
just because she says so.

BIRTHDAY PRESENT

Like me, you've been

dying your hair for so long
that the natural color is a mystery
of earth beneath concrete, each dead
weed through the sidewalk a color somewhere
between mouse and straw, but it's taken
care of before we're sure. Like me, you have long,
long fingers that make people tell you
to learn piano, but mama would never fall
for something like that. And like me, you have

Botticelli lids that drop down
in photos, making your eyes look like two white
slits, rolled back, stoned. But this is all
I know—not your favorite
color or dinner or show, not
the name of this crush or that,
not the sound of your laugh that makes
you easy to spot in a crowd.
What is enough

to bind us? Is blood really thicker
than? And now that you know this
story, my half on the other side
of the tracks and your father a train,
ripping through town, do you claim me?
What courses through is enough
to tether me, reaching back to salvage
this wreck, run with my blinders torn
off and trampled in the mud. I want nothing

but truth between us, but I am afraid.
Last night I cut myself
wrapping your birthday present, pollacking
the paper with red, my finger
refusing its right to not stop bleeding
until morning, and even when it did
the slit kept pulsing like your anger
that tries to be polite
given a gift that's way late,
two sizes too small, outgrown
by years, a stupid thing given
by someone who should know better.

STRADDLING FENCES

Sister, I've tried it all.
Gardening, yoga, therapy, you name it—
I've smoked my house out
with incense, taped prayers to the inside
of my fridge, worn my fingernails
clipped and bare, neglected

the bottle of pink polish
gumming on the windowsill.
I've tried pills and red wine;
I've thought of the sawed-off
shotgun under mama's bed, of the slow
release of red into a tub, of twisting the white
tulle scallops of my canopy
into a rope to hang myself there.

I've traveled, trying to leave it
behind—heels squeaking on ancient marble,
dolphins chasing my boat on a flat sea,
boys with eyes that spun like bicycle wheels
in rain. I left my first husband, my one
true home, then moved into an empty house
comforted by the nothing

of waxed hardwood floors. I have eaten
turnip greens sautéed with virgin oil,
simple food we never heard of growing up
like sushi, basmati, butternut squash.
But I still drink soda every morning,
and when I'm sick, it's straight
to the fried comfort,
a bottle of hot sauce nearby.

How can I make all this fit? How did I
make it through? Our mama in
therapy makes about as much sense
as putting Buddha in the seat of that car
we used to go to in the woods, that rusted-out Ford
of creeping charlie vine and bullet holes,
the base of a bottle all the kids said
was broken off in somebody.
Sitting there on that dry-rot

driver's seat, our hands on the crusted
wheel, was a terror so beautiful
we never thought of going anywhere.
I had to try something, had to leave
you behind, had to try to be thankful
for the chance to boss my way
through the city gates, switching all the time
between *isn't* and *ain't*, my feet
in designer red heels
with creek mud still between my toes.

Straddling a fence, I think mama would say.
On one side,
rusting barbwire, a tree swing, the green smell
of cow patties in the sun.
On the other,
another me,
pressed,
dressed,
right as fucking rain.

THE RED WARBLER'S CHILD

I've shed my skin
for the cuckoo
again and again, littering the ground
with so many selves it's like cicada
season, another seven-year brood
to crunch underfoot,
their shells empty and dry.

I can't stop to think: whose baby
am I suckling? And what has been pushed
to the ground? What husband, what babies,
what window boxes in full bloom? What bone
china and fresh sheets from the dryer and red
tricycle rainshining in the drive?
Don't ask, because my chance of family
is yolk and pink tissue strung
across this garden floor.

I am just a red warbler, fetching
larvae for the past
I never wanted to call my own.
I sit down and do
what I am told. I answer when it calls,
no questions asked, no
questions asked.

INVITATION

Come over Saturday. Drop your
sloppy satchel of books at my front door
and wear that blue shade of eyeliner
that you are not yet too old to wear. We'll shop
pointy-toed shoes, push-up bras, summer
tees, low rise jeans, then fry up
chicken, pickles, potato. We'll rent a movie
we don't agree on, sit next to each other
on the couch and I'll notice
your nails—white keratin, bitten down
moons; nervous and your knees drawn up, rocking
gently to the edge. I'll pretend
there's this fast one, his hand sliding up,
his name all over your locker.
Another maybe who is tall enough
to hunch, his shoulders sad in doorways,
a note folded into a triangle
pretend football kick flicked into the air.

But don't worry. I won't ask.
I won't say to you, *wait.*
I won't say, *listen.*
I won't say *yes, it's true, your father.*
I won't say *your coming into this world was the honey*
in the rock, a fontanel
of baking bread, an ache placed squarely
in my throat, a lesson of why to stay,
when to go. I won't say *wait, let me tell you, let me*
show you, here is your origin, your pillow flipped,
your heartbeat bassinet, your long white hall
of welcome that was never guarded
by ghosts. I won't say

you have just begun, you have not begun
ending.

No, sister, there is warm
silence here, a smile, a gesture. I'll say,
pass the popcorn, dork-o, and you'll smile.
I'll say, *cute shoes* and you'll stretch
your bare feet before you and put them on before
you go.

BIOGRAPHICAL NOTE

Nickole Brown graduated from the M.F.A. Program for Creative Writing at Vermont College and has received grants from the Kentucky Foundation for Women and the Kentucky Arts Council. She studied English Literature at Oxford University as an English Speaking Union Scholar and worked as an editorial assistant for the late Hunter S. Thompson. Her work has appeared in *The Courtland Review, Diagram Magazine, Another Chicago Magazine, Chautauqua Literary Journal, 32 Poems, The Kestrel Review, The Writer's Chronicle, Poets & Writers,* and the anthologies *Sudden Stories* and *PP/FF*. She also co-edited the anthology, *Air Fare: Stories, Poems, & Essays on Flight*. Nickole lives in Louisville, Kentucky, where she works at the independent literary press, Sarabande Books.